![NATIONAL GEOGRAPHIC OUR WORLD]

The Green Rabbit

A Fairy Tale from Mexico

Retold by Cindy Pioli

T0349316

NATIONAL GEOGRAPHIC LEARNING | CENGAGE Learning®

Long ago in Mexico, a pretty girl named Marisol walked in the forest near her home. As she walked, she sang.

Her singing was so beautiful, the forest animals came close to hear it.

One of the animals was a big, green rabbit.

The rabbit hopped right up to Marisol.
"A green rabbit!" she said. "How amazing!"
The rabbit followed Marisol through the
forest. It even followed her to her home.
"You are the cutest rabbit!" said Marisol.

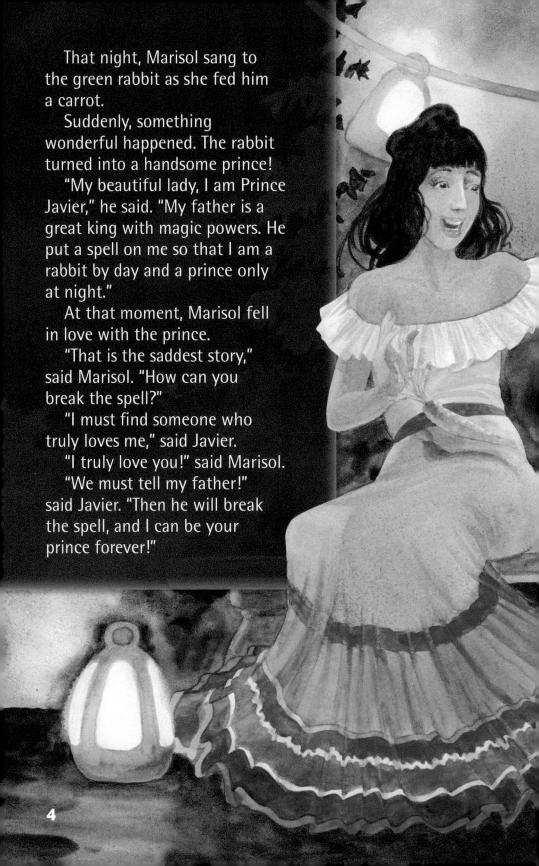

That night, Marisol sang to the green rabbit as she fed him a carrot.

Suddenly, something wonderful happened. The rabbit turned into a handsome prince!

"My beautiful lady, I am Prince Javier," he said. "My father is a great king with magic powers. He put a spell on me so that I am a rabbit by day and a prince only at night."

At that moment, Marisol fell in love with the prince.

"That is the saddest story," said Marisol. "How can you break the spell?"

"I must find someone who truly loves me," said Javier.

"I truly love you!" said Marisol.

"We must tell my father!" said Javier. "Then he will break the spell, and I can be your prince forever!"

The next day, Marisol and Javier went to the palace.

At the palace, Marisol talked to the king.

"I love your son," she said. "Please break the spell and let him stay a prince."

"Javier is my favorite child," said the king. "You can not just tell me you love him. You must show me. I will give you two tests to prove your love."

"First, fill this barrel with your tears and bring it to me," said the king. "After that, I will give you the second test."

Then the king picked Javier
up, and they disappeared.

Without Javier, Marisol was very sad. She cried for many days. Soon, she filled the barrel with her tears. She brought the barrel back to the palace.

"Very good," said the king. "You passed the first test. You are ready for the second test. You must wear out these six pairs of boots."

Marisol took the boots. She put on one pair, and she started to walk.

Marisol walked for days and days. She walked through villages, towns, and cities.

Marisol wore out all of the boots. But now she was far away from the king's palace.

9

"I traveled so far from Javier.
How can I get back to him?"
she cried.

The Summer Wind heard
Marisol. He picked her up with
her sack full of worn-out boots.
He carried her over villages,
towns, and cities.

He took her back to the
king's palace.

Marisol showed the boots to the king.

The king smiled. "You truly do love my son," he said. The king broke the spell and turned the green rabbit back into Prince Javier.

Marisol and Javier got married and lived a wonderful, long, and happy life together.

Facts About Beauty

Many fairy tales include beautiful princesses and handsome princes. But what is beauty?

Long ago, artists and scientists had an idea about what made some things more beautiful than others. They called this idea the **golden ratio**.

The golden ratio describes a rectangular space, also called a golden rectangle, which has a length slightly more than one and a half times its width. This ratio is described in math as 1:1.618. This ratio is everywhere in nature. It can be found in plants, flowers, seashells, insects, and parts of the human body.

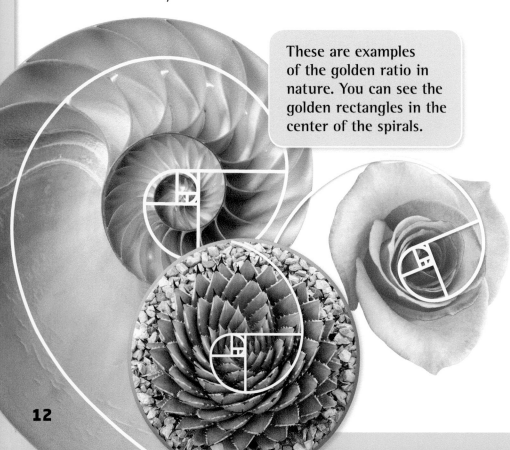

These are examples of the golden ratio in nature. You can see the golden rectangles in the center of the spirals.

The golden ratio in the Parthenon

Ancient builders used the golden ratio to make beautiful buildings like the Parthenon in Greece.

Artists used the golden ratio to create beauty in their paintings of people. The faces in these paintings are about one and a half times longer than they are wide. Many people think this makes the people look beautiful or handsome.

The golden ratio in paintings by Leonardo da Vinci (above) and Diego Rodríguez de Silva y Velázquez (above, right)

The faces of popular and beautiful movie stars often show the golden ratio, too. Still, different people have different ideas about what looks beautiful. That's what makes the world such an interesting place!

Fun with Adjectives

What word describes each person or thing? Complete each sentence with the correct word.

popular	pretty	interesting	handsome

1. Eliza has many friends.
She is ___popular___ .

2. Baron has a good-looking face.
He is _____ .

3. Sheila has beautiful hair.
It is _____ .

4. The book isn't boring.
It is _____ .

Find and circle the words in the puzzle.

great	amazing	handsome	interesting
popular	pretty	wonderful	

T	N	F	S	L	P	R	E	T	T	Y	J
Y	I	J	H	U	E	U	Z	R	L	Y	P
B	N	N	A	C	T	K	A	K	R	K	A
B	T	L	N	W	M	L	M	Y	N	M	Y
P	E	D	D	W	U	M	A	K	B	P	J
E	R	Z	S	P	F	P	Z	A	W	M	Q
P	E	K	O	H	C	J	I	S	J	T	S
M	S	P	M	S	L	E	N	B	A	R	H
O	T	E	E	F	W	V	G	E	O	R	G
G	I	W	O	N	D	E	R	F	U	L	V
Q	N	R	Y	U	K	G	E	G	W	W	Q
L	G	F	D	A	M	G	H	N	X	G	B

What do you think makes someone pretty or handsome? Write a paragraph that tells your opinion. Use a bilingual dictionary if necessary.

Glossary

barrel

barrel a large, round container made of wood

disappeared was suddenly not seen anymore

moment a very small period of time

palace

palace a large building where a king or a queen lives

passed did well on a test

powers abilities to do something or make something happen

prove to show the truth of something

put a spell on to use magic to change someone or something into something else

tears

tears the liquid that comes from the eyes when someone cries

truly really

turned into became

wear out to use something until it falls apart